THE DI SABATINO LIFE STORY

OUR JOURNEY AND STORY OF TRIALS, TRIBULATIONS, VICTORIES AND MIRACLES.

By Moses Di Sabatino

THE DI SABATINO LIFE STORY

Copyright © 2021 MOSES DI SABATINO

All rights reserved.

Deeper Life Press

I dedicate this book first to the memory of my
parents,

GIUSEPPE DI SABATINO, 1896-1982

SOFIA DI SABATINO, 1902-1993

who gave me a cherished legacy: to believe that
character and integrity are more valuable than
wealth and that what we possess is less
important than what kind of people we are.

I also dedicate this book to the memory of my
wife who helped shape my life by living an
exemplary godly life.

MARIA PIA DI SABATINO, 1940-2015

I further dedicate this book to my two sons,
Daniel and Sandro and their respective wives,
Kelly and Rebecca, my six grand-children and to
my three great-grand-children who bring me
more joy than I ever imagined.

I truly hope I will leave them a legacy that will
help them be all God created them to be.

TABLE OF CONTENTS

Introduction
TO THE DI SABATINO PROJECT

◆

My father was 44 years of age and my mother 38 when I was born. At that point, they had already experienced good and bad experiences interwoven with trials, tribulations, tests, victories and miracles. Then they faced both world wars as well as the terrible Great Depression of the 1930's that lasted approximatly ten years.

The entire family dealt with **diphtheria pandemic,** especially the young people, including all my brothers and sisters, but gave thanks to the Lord for His incredible healing power.

They courageously faced family tragedies, including the death of several beloved children.

There is a quote that says *"No parent should have to bury a child."* My parents buried three.

During their lifetimes, they also experienced victories and saw firsthand miracles, with people being saved, healed from their infirmities, and delivered from demonic spirits. God moved mightily, demonstrating his power in ways most people never see. [El Elyon "The Most High God"]

The most meaningful miracle of all was the transformation of my father's life.

I pray that this story of my father would bless the reader, "that a people not yet created may praise the Lord." Ps. 102:18.

The Di Sabatino
LIFE STORY PROJECT

We have heard with our ears, O God;

Our father has told us what you did in their days.
Psalm 44:1

I will speak, I will tell things, things of old, what I have heard and known, What our father have told us, (*things I have seen with my own eyes*)

I will not keep them from our children, We will tell the next generatioin about the Lord's Power And his deeds and the wonderful things he has done.

He instructed our ancestors to teach his laws to their children, Even the children yet to be born and they in turn would tell their children.

In this way they also will put their trust in God and not forget what he has Done but always obey his commandaments.
Psalm 78: 2-7. (paraprased)

Let this be written for a future generation, that a people not yet created
may praise the Lord.
Psalm 102:18

My Father Giuseppe Di Sabatino was born July 10, 1896, to Antonio Di Sabatino and Elisabetta Completa Di Sabatino in Castelli, Teramo, Italy, a small village in the central area of the province of Teramo, Abruzzo, Italy. The tiny town was nestled in the beautiful and majestic Mountain Grand Sasso (Big Rock), the highest peak in the Apennines mountains reaching 2912 meters (9,553 feet) above sea-level and forming part of the mountain chain that stretches from northern Italy to the most southern part of the "Boot."

Castelli is a *commune* in the province of Teramo, Abruzzo, Italy, included in the Gran Sasso e Monti della Laga National Park.

The medieval hill town lies beneath Mount Camicia on the eastern side of the Gran Sasso Massif. Castelli is best known for decorative ceramic majolica items, which were most sought after by European nobility from the sixteenth through eighteenth centuries and are still produced today by local artists. Castelli majolica was also the favorite dinnerware of Russian Tsars.

One of the most valued collections of Castelli ceramics is now housed at the Winter Palace of the Hermitage State Museum in St. Petersburg, Russia. Castelli's main church is San Donato, which holds a majolica altar-piece by Francesco Grue (1647) and a medieval silver cross is on display at the Sulmona school. Its tiled ceiling is believed to have been decorated by the ceramics master Oracio Pompei or artists working out of his studio.

Today, Castelli hosts an art institute and ceramics museum as well as many popular ceramics shops and studios.NOTE:

My cousin Dino Mercante was a professor/ teacher of majolica/ceramics at the institute of arts in Castelli

Casteli located central/east of Italy

Village in Abruzzo, Italy

Village of Castelli,Abruzzo

My father's siblings included brothers Nicola and Eugenio and one sister, Rita. Below is a picture of Dad's family including uncle Nicola and Uncle Eugenion, circa 1950

First row from left to right: my brother Antonio, my sister Maria, my mom, my dad, uncle Eugenio, uncle Nicola, my sister Nella, my brother Luciano. Second row, Me (Moses), my grandmother Elisabetta, my brother Samuel.

Moses, mom, dad, circa 1961

At the age of sixteen [1912] Giuseppe emigrated to Brantford, Ontario, Canada where he lived for nearly ten years.

In 1922, at the age twenty-six he returned to Italy for a visit, fully intending to return to Canada, but no sooner had he arrived in Italy when the government closed immigration, so that he was unable to return to Canada until 1960, some thirty-eight years later.

Italy had been the site of much warfare during the First World War and was still suffering from the ravages of the war. Government was unstable, work was scarce, unemployment was at its peak, and living conditions were desperate. The education system was nearly nonexistent. As a result, illiteracy and poverty were rampant, forcing people to search for alternatives. With no other options many people were forced to emigrate to different parts of the world.

But Giuseppe still dreamt of returning to Canada with his family. Believing he had a better chance of emigrating to Canada from South America, he was fifty years old when he made plans to move to Montevideo, Uraguay. For nine months he tried unsuccessfully to emigrate to Canada, before he made the move back home to Italy.

Life in Canada

The only photo available of my father, circa 1915 when he was in Canada the first time.

Dad arrived in Brantford Ontario in the middle of winter where he was faced with the usual Canadian winter, including lots of snow, ice and penetrating wind, but even frigid weather couldn't dampen his enthusiasm for his new home, where he felt right at home. In fact, Italy's winters were just as cold, and at least Canadian homes had central heat, while Italian homes depended on fireplaces or wood burning stoves for heat, for those who could afford them at all.

In a short time, he found a permanent job with a local foundry where he took pride in his work in building maintenance, which then paved the way for continual promotions, so that in the end, he was put in charge of his own specialized department, a position he held until his return to Italy.

During that time, he became known as a leader and savvy business man in the community.

After saving up the funds, he purchased a Harley Davidson motorcycle—probably the only one in Brantford at that time. (Wonder why a *HARLEY/DAVIDSON MOTORCYCLE?*)

1912/13 Harley/Davidson

1917 Harley/Davidson

1918 Harley/Davidson

He didn't talk much about his personal life in Canada, but we know he was a Roman Catholic, who only attended services a couple of times a year, on Christmas and Easter.

The Return
AND LIFE IN ITALY

D ad was twenty-six years old when he returned to Italy in 1922, and after a reality check, when he realized he couldn't go back to Canada, he settled in his hometown of Castelli.

There he purchased a small farm just outside Castelli, consisting of a small acreage of workable land that included a wooded area with a brook that descended from the Grand Sasso mountain. Soon he married a beautiful woman by the name of Sofia Mercante, and together they made their home on the farm.

Over the next eighteen years, they had a total of nine children. First came Elisabetta, followed by

Maria, Antonio, Guido, Luciano, Nella, Ester, Mose' and Samuele. Unfortunately, only six of them grew to adulthood.

The first born, Elisabetta, died at age fourteen, Guido died at three months old, and Ester died when she was twenty-seven months old.

The farm wasn't big enough to provide for the needs of the growing family, so he saw a need and filled it, opening up a plant that manufactured charcoal, which was in very short supply at the time.

The wooded section of his land became the backdrop for the manufacturing process. After being licensed by the government to cut the trees, he, as the collier (professional charcoal maker) hired a team of laborers to split the trees into one-to-four-inch widths called lap wood and four-to-seven-inch pieces known as billets that were processed into charcoal. As the owner of this enterprise Giuseppe's reputation grew along with his business.

Below is a bit of history of the wood charcoal manufacturing business. Historically, the production of wood charcoal took place where there was an abundance of wood and

generally consisted of piling billets of wood on their ends in order to form a conical pile, with openings left at the bottom to admit air, with a central shaft to serve as a flue.

The whole pile is then covered with turf or moistened clay. The firing begins at the bottom of the flue, and gradually spreads up and out. The success of the operation depends upon the rate of combustion. Under average conditions, the operation is so delicate that it is left to colliers (professional charcoal burners), in order to produce a good quality product.

The Big Transformation and
THE BEGINNING OF NEW LIFE

Like most of the population of Italy, my parents and especially my mother, were moderately religious Catholics, who seldom attended church and had little regard for God, except to take his name in vain.

From the outside, the family appeared to be doing well, living on a little farm with a thriving business and healthy, happy children. In fact, from all appearances, it seemed they had arrived, but behind the scenes, few outsiders ever saw the emptiness, unrest and dissatisfaction that was the hallmark of family life there.

When my dad first left Italy for Canada, someone on the ship gave him a little booklet that he tucked away with his important papers and forgot. Years after he returned to Italy he came across that booklet where he read the following scripture passage.

"Come to me, all you who are weary and burdened, and I will give you rest. Take my yoke upon you and learn from me, for I am gentle and humble in heart, and you will find rest for your souls. For my yoke is easy and my burden is light." (Matthew 11:28-30)

Though he couldn't grasp the meaning of the statement, it piqued his curiosity, inspiring him to search for someone who could help him understand it.

At that time Dad knew a man, whose name was Carmine Di Claudio, who had recently returned from Philadelphia, Pennsylvania, USA to his native village of Castelli. Rumor had it that Carmine had undergone a life-changing experience, even becoming an "evangelist" (locals used the term in a derogatory way), because he had jumped ship from Catholicism to Protestantism. Ignoring the neighborhood criticism, Dad eagerly sought him out to explain the message of the booklet.

For Carmine Di Claudio, the transformation was a defining moment that changed everything.*

To quote the man himself: "It was an encounter with the living Jesus, the Son of God, where I experienced and obtained *rest for my soul and peace from my weary and burdensome heart and forgiveness of my sins.*"

*<u>The Saul of Tarsus Experience.</u>

In Scripture, we find that Saul of Tarsus was a brilliant young Jewish man educated under Gamaliel, one of the best professors in the school of law of that day. There he'd been taught that anything that disagreed with those teachings was heretical and needed to be stomped out. From Saul's point of view, everything was black or white. He believed it was his life's mission to persecute Christians, whom he believed were heretics. In fact, he had been authorized by the Council and chief priests to jail Christians and even put some of them to death.

But God had a different plan for Saul of Tarsus, which he reported to King Agrippa, as recorded in Acts chapters 9-26.

(You can read the Saul's conversion full story in Acts 9: 1-19, 22: 1-16, 26: 9-18)

[12] *"On one of these journeys I was going to Damascus with the authority and commission of the chief priests.* [13] *About noon, King Agrippa, as I was on the road, I saw a light from heaven, brighter than the sun, blazing around me and my companions.*

[14] *We all fell to the ground, and I heard a voice saying to me in Aramaic 'Saul, Saul, why do you persecute me? It is hard for you to kick against the goads.'*

[15] *"Then I asked, 'Who are you, Lord?'*
'I am Jesus, whom you are persecuting,' the Lord replied. [16] *'Now get up and stand on your feet. I have appeared to you to appoint you as a servant and as a witness of what you have seen and will see of me.* [17] *I will rescue you from your own people and from the Gentiles. I am sending you to them* [18] *to open*

their eyes and turn them from darkness to light, and from the power of Satan to God, so that they may receive forgiveness of sins and a place among those who are sanctified by faith in me.'

Saul's transformation was stunning; he had gone from a "murderer to a preacher who taught that Jesus is the Son of God and forgiver of sins."

In the same way Carmine became a new man and had the urge to go back to his native village of Castelli to share "the born-again experience" with family, and friends.

Dad met with Carmine, who explained that peace and rest could be found only in a personal relationship with Christ as Savior. Carmine then explained the story of the fall of Adam and Eve, who disobeyed by eating from the forbidden Tree of the Knowledge of the Knowledge of Good and Evil, forever changing the dynamic between God and mankind for all time. He went on to explain that sin had left a huge chasm in man's relationship with God, for all time. But God had a plan to restore all that was lost, in order to redeem mankind as we read in John 3:16: "God so loved the world (all mankind) that whoever believes in him shall not perish but have eternal life." (Emphasis mine.)

⁸ Now the LORD God had planted a garden in the east, in Eden; and there he put the man he had formed. ⁹ The LORD God made all kinds of trees grow out of the ground—trees that were pleasing to the eye and good for food. In the middle of the garden were the tree of life and the tree of the knowledge of good and evil.

¹⁵ The LORD God took the man and put him in the Garden of Eden to work it and take care of it. ¹⁶ And the LORD God commanded the man, "You are free to eat from any tree in the garden; ¹⁷ but you must not eat from the tree of the knowledge of good and evil, **"for when you eat from it you will certainly die."** *Genesis 2: 8-, 15-17.*

(You will find this story in Genesis 3:1-24)

That night my father realized he was a sinner, asked forgiveness and accepted Jesus Christ as his personal Savior and Lord of his life.

Immediately he felt the presence of God filling his heart with such love that "the terrible feeling of emptiness, unrest, and dissatisfaction disappeared once and for all."

At that point, he thoroughly understood the meaning of the "quote" in the "famous" booklet:

"Come to me, all you who are weary and burdened, and I will give you rest. Take my yoke upon you and learn from me, for I am gentle and humble in heart, and you will find rest for your souls. For my yoke is easy and my burden is light." (Matthew 11:28-30

From Physical Abuser

TO LOVING HUSBAND

After meeting with di Claudio, Dad returned home a completely different man. Most nights he had spent getting drunk at a bar before going home to quarrel with his wife. It would inevitably escalate to physical abuse. But that night, he burst into uncontrollable weeping, to the stunned surprise of his wife, who couldn't believe what she was seeing.

At first, she assumed he wept after being beaten, but when he explained that he'd had an encounter with Jesus, she wanted no part of it. It didn't matter to her that he was now a humble man, broken, loving and weeping instead of drunk and abusive.

He spent most of the night prostrate on the floor, talking and listening to God and thanking Him for the freedom, peace and rest he found in Jesus. That very night he received a call to ministry, to preach the gospel to all who had ears to hear.

Sharing the Good News with the family

The very next morning, he gathered the whole family around the breakfast table, including my mother and her five children, Dad's parents plus his brothers Nicola and Eugenio and their families. In the presence of twenty people, he explained his new relationship with Jesus, and invited them to be saved. With the exception of my mother, every single family member fell to their knees sobbing, and invited Jesus into their hearts. In front of everyone, my mother shook her head and said she had no use for this new religion, because she was Catholic and would always be a Catholic.

She had always been a very single-minded individual, but she had no idea that the Holy Spirit had other plans for her future. In fact, He wooed her heart, so that in a short time, she, too, gave her life to the Lord. Over time, she became a strong and godly woman and a wonderful helpmeet to my father, the pastor. Over the years she won many to the Lord, after sharing how He transformed her from a religious person to someone who knew Jesus as an intimate personal friend.

The following event occurred twelve years after my father's move home from Canada. (1933)

The Born Again
EXPERIENCE

What my father and mother and the rest of the Di Sabatino "clan" experienced is referred in the Bible as "Born Again Experience."

In Roman 9:10-13 we read:

"⁹ If you confess with your mouth, "that Jesus is Lord," and believe in your heart that God raised him from the dead, you will be saved. ¹⁰ For it is with your heart that you believe and are justified, and it is with your mouth that you confess your faith and are saved.

¹³ "Everyone who calls on the name of the Lord will be saved.

Acts 4:12 also declares:
*"Salvation **is** found in **no** one else, for **there is no other name** under heaven given to mankind by which we must be saved."*

In John 3:3 Jesus declared:
"Very truly I tell you, no one can see the kingdom of God unless they are "BORN AGAIN."

This process is a distinct experience, an identifiable moment in time when, by faith, a person simply and sincerely trusts and accepts Jesus Christ as personal Savior.

That particular morning the Di Sabatinos had that "distinct and Identifiable moment" when they confessed their sins, asked for forgiveness, believed and accepted Jesus Christ, the Son of God as their Savior and the Lord of their lives. At that moment they were **saved**, they were **"born again," and became new creatures in Christ.**

Life Before
THE "BORN AGAIN EXPERIENCE"

As mentioned earlier, Giuseppe's family was living in Italy during and after World War One, when the country was still reeling from the ravages of war. The government was unstable, work was scarce and unemployment numbers broke all records. Education had suffered, so that illiteracy was very high and poverty was the order of the day. Unrelated families joined with other families, living under the same roof, and they would work together, pooling all their resources in order to survive.

The Di Sabatino family clan was no different. At that time, the family unit included one sister, Rita, who married and moved far from Castelli, thirty plus kilometers from Castelli, to start her own family. Travel was difficult back then, so, from that time on, Rita had little contact with her family. Back in Castelli, there were two remaining brothers, Nicola and Eugenio besides Giuseppe, who was fortunate enough to own a small farm where they raised food crops that kept them from starvation.

Both Nicola and Eugenio married, but neither of them had much work, and ended up doing menial work that paid very little.

With no other options, my father eventually took in his brothers and their families, so that twenty people lived and worked together in the small farmhouse in Castelli, serving each other and the Lord.

The War Years

Italy and the rest of the world went through 2 World Wars in the span of thirty-one years as well as the Great Depression that lasted ten plus years, from 1929 to 1939.

They lived through the First World War * (WW1), from July 28, 1914 to November 11, 2018, (4 years, 3 months and 2 weeks)

Then they struggled to get through the Second World War ** (WW11) from September 1, 1939 to September 2, 1945. (6 years and 1 day) and through the "Great Depression"*** (1929 to 1939.)

*World War I (or the First World War, often abbreviated as WWI or WW1) was a global war originating in Europe, that lasted from July 28, 1914 to November 11 of 1918. Contemporaneously known as the Great War or "the war to end all wars",[7] it led to the mobilization of more than 70 million military personnel, including 60 million Europeans, making it one of the largest wars in history.[8][9] It also was one of the deadliest conflicts in history,[10] with an estimated 8.5 million combatant deaths and 13 million civilian deaths as a direct result of the war,[11] while resulting genocides and the related 1918 Spanish flu pandemic caused another 17–100 million deaths worldwide,[12][13] including an estimated 2.64 million Spanish flu deaths in Europe and as many as 675,000 Spanish flu deaths in the United States.

World War II or the **Second World War**, often abbreviated as **WWII** or **WW2**, was a global war that lasted from 1939 to 1945. It involved the vast majority of the world's countries—including all the great powers—forming two opposing military alliances: the Allies and the Axis. In a state of total war, directly involving more than 100 million personnel from more than 30 countries, the major participants threw their entire economic, industrial, and scientific capabilities behind the war effort, blurring the distinction between civilian and military resources. World War II was the deadliest conflict in human history, resulting in 70 to 85 million fatalities, with more civilians than military personnel killed. Tens of millions of people died due to genocides (including the Holocaust), premeditated death from starvation, massacres, and disease. Aircraft played a major role in the conflict, including in strategic bombing of population centers, and the development of nuclear weapons.

*** The **Great Depression** was a severe worldwide economic depression that took place mostly during the 1930s, beginning in the United States. The timing of the Great Depression varied across the world; in most countries, it started in 1929 and lasted until the late thirties.[1] It was the longest, deepest, and most widespread depression of the 20th Century.[2] The Great Depression is commonly used as an example of how quickly and intensely the global economy can decline.[3]

The Great Depression started in the United States after a major fall in stock prices that began around September 4, 1929, and became worldwide news with the stock market crash of October 29, 1929, (known as Black Tuesday). Between 1929 and 1932, the worldwide gross domestic product (GDP) fell by an estimated 15%. By comparison, worldwide GDP fell by less than 1% from 2008 to 2009 during the Great Recession.[4] Some economies started to recover by the mid-1930s. However, in many countries, the negative effects of the Great Depression lasted until the beginning of World War II.[5]

The Great Depression had devastating effects in both rich and poor countries. Personal income, tax revenue, profits and prices dropped, while international trade fell by more than 50%. Unemployment in the U.S. rose to 23% and in some countries rose as high as 33%.[6]

Big cities around the world were hard hit, especially those dependent on heavy industry. Construction was virtually halted in many countries. Farming communities and rural areas suffered as crop prices fell by about 60%.[7][8][9] Facing plummeting demand with few alternative sources for jobs, areas dependent on primary sector industries such as mining and logging suffered the most.

The Call
TO SERVICE

In Castelli there was a group of born-again believers who had formed a church where they met for worship, Bible study and prayer, led by pastor/evangelist Carmine Di Claudio.

My dad and the rest of the "Disabatino Clan" joined this group and as result they were growing in the faith and in the knowledge of God through the reading and studying of the Bible.
But God was preparing my dad for a special call to pastoral and evangelistic service to fulfill the call on his life.

My dad's heart was tender toward people who were weary, heavily burdened, and lost in sin—especially those who wanted to be free and find rest for their souls. He was especially eager to answer the Scripture passage found in Mark 16:15-18:

[15] He (Jesus) said to them, (the disciples) "Go into all the world and preach the gospel to all creation. [16] Whoever believes and is baptized will be saved, but whoever does not believe will be condemned. [17] And these signs will accompany those who believe: In my name they will drive out demons; they will speak in new tongues; [18] they will pick up snakes with their hands; and when they drink deadly poison, it will not hurt them at all; they will place their hands on sick people, and they will get well.

****** <u>A word about the Call.</u>**

God called and is still calling men and women of different races, both those who are well educated, and those with no education, from a wide range of different professions, ages, whether rich or poor, just as He has since the beginning of time. This number included men like:

<u>-Noah:</u> called to build an ark, "He did everything just as God commended him."

-<u>Moses</u>: called while he was tending the flock of his father-in-law Jethro, to deliver the Israelites from slavery of Egypt.

-<u>Samuel</u>: called to become a Prophet-Priest.

-<u>David</u>: called while minding his father's sheep when "Samuel anointed him as King."

-<u>Isaiah</u>: "The greatest of the writing prophets."

<u>Jesus called his disciples: mostly fishermen, but also tax collectors</u>:

-Simon, also called Peter,
-Andrew: Peter's brother
-James;
-John: James brother,
-Philip,
-Bartholomew,
-Thomas,
-Matthew: tax collector,
-James: son of Alphaeus
-Simon: the Zealot,
-Judas: son of James,

-Judas Iscariot: who betrayed Jesus.

Note that four of his followers were called James, (which must have been a very common name at that time.)

-<u>Saul of Tarsus:</u> "The persecutor and murderer of the Christians, transformed into a disciple of Christ" and an Apostle, who wrote 13 epistles (letters) plus letters to the churches of the New Testament.

To this very day, God has continued to call men and women to diverse ministries including as Evangelists, Preachers, Missionaries, Ministers of the Gospel, Counselors, Authors, Theologians, Writers of Christian literature, Song writers, Publishers, etc. men and women like Fanny Crosby, Charles H. Spurgeon, Dwight L. Moody, Karl Barth, C. S. Lewis, Joni Eareckson Tada, Billy Graham, just to mention a few, and in the same way, God called "Giuseppe Di Sabatino, Evangelist/Pastor, a Minister of the Gospel."

The church in Castelli already had a pastor/evangelist in the person of Carmine Di

Claudio and the work was going fairly well, so Castelli didn't need another pastor.

But God began stirring my father's heart to move to another area of the province and start a new work there. In response to the "tugging on his heart" he decided to liquidate his assets and prepare for the move, "but where was he to go?"

God orchestrated a series of events, and miracles started to happen.

Between WW1 and WW11, the economy began to improve somewhat, however work was still scarce and hard to find.

There was one possibility for the 3 Di Sabatino brothers to get into the work force, and work toward better living conditions.

Sharecropping
(MEZZADRIA IN ITALIAN)

What does a sharecropper do for a living?

Sharecropping is a form of agriculture in which a landowner allows the sharecropper to farm the land that belongs to a landowner. The sharecropping family would plow, plant, weed, and harvest the land in return for a share of the crops the land produced.

Giuseppe began to search for such sharecropping farms, and found two farms available, one in Tossicia and one in Montorio al Vomano, a distance of between 20 to 30 Km from Caselli, and 9-10 Km from Tossicia.

A family decision was made to enter into contract with both farms where they applied and both contracts were approved and accepted. The 3 Di Sabatino brothers decided that Giuseppe would work Montorio while families Nicola and Eugenio and their families would combine their efforts to work the Tossicia farm.

Funds were scarce for Nicola and Eugenio brothers, so my father provided the funds to his brothers to purchase the needed equipment and machinery to work the land and to set up a living quarters and purchase necessities for his brothers' families.

A moving date was scheduled and the move was on, in 1933 Giuseppe's family moved to Montorio while his brothers moved to Tossicia.

Tossicia (Abruzzese: *Tussëcië*) is a town and *commune* in the province of Teramo in the Abruzzo region of central/eastern Italy. It is located in the natural park known as the "Gran Sasso e Monti della Laga National Park."

In the dark years of World War II, Tossicia was the site of a concentration camp, active from October 21 of 1940 to September 26, 1943.

Tossicia, view of South/West

Tossicia, view part of the Grand Sasso

Montorio al Vomano (Abruzzese: *Mundurje*) is a town and *commune* in the province of Teramo, in the Abruzzo region of central-southern Italy. It is located in the natural park known as the Gran Sasso e Monti della Laga National Park.

Montorio al Vomano

A New Beginning
IN A NEW AND STRANGE COMMUNITY

Things in Tossicia were going fairly well for the two brothers, but not so well for my dad in Montorio.

It started out well but soon the relationship deteriorated between my dad and the landowner, who began to impose hefty requirements contrary to the legally-signed sharecropping contract.

With no other options, as result of breach of contract, my father resigned and the contract was terminated.

Meanwhile, as an answer to prayer, and definitely God's master plan for my father's call, a sharecropping farm became available in Tossicia, so Dad didn't waste any time, and after he did his "due diligence", he entered in to a contract with new farm owner.

So, in 1934, Giuseppe finished the farming season in Montorio and prepared to move his wife, Sofia and their five children to the new farm in Tossicia.

Incidentally, the farm in Tossicia, consisted of approximately 6 hectares (approximately 14 acres) of workable land that included a forest, and was located approximately 2 Km from the farm of his brothers Nicola and Eugenio. Soon the three families were reunited in the same area within walking distance of each other, but each on his own farm.

Life in Tossicia

My father's farm was located approximately 1-2 Km just south of Tossicia, with an outstanding vista of the village and a breathtaking view of rolling farm lands to the north/east, and to the south/west and tremendous view of the majestic Mountain Grand Sasso (Big Rock) with the highest peak reaching 2912 Meters (9,553 feet) above sea-level in the Apennines mountains forming part of the chain that stretches from north Italy to the most southern part of the "Boot."

Vista   South /West   South/West
North/East

Tossicia is a unique village with a population of 1418 (2011), 2780 (1951), 2644 (1931),

It's clear that the population has been declining over the years, mostly for lack of "things to do." With nearly no resources in Tossicia, it has become a "sleepy town."

It has a city hall, an elementary school, the high school, a pharmacy, a family doctor, a Catholic church, a soccer team, and at one time it even housed the local court system.

The residents of Tossicia, especially the men, are very proud inhabitants (though I don't understand why--probably because I" was born there?? (Not likely.) For whatever reason, they love the village, referring to themselves with pride as the *"Tussëciënaes"* a locally used word used to describe the inhabitants of Tossicia.

as the *"Tussëciënaes"* a locally used word used to describe the inhabitants of Tossicia.

Life on The Farm
IN TOSSICIA

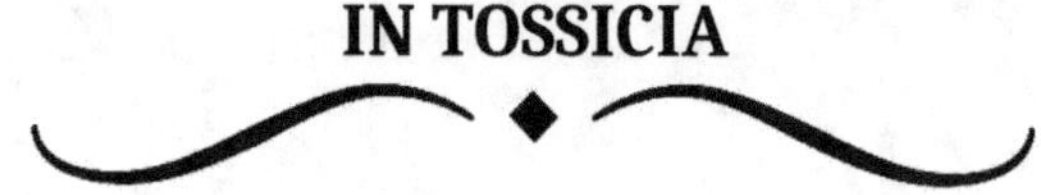

After they settled in at the farm, they soon found out the land had not been cultivated or taken care of. Once they'd done a quick assessment, they realised they were in for a lot of work, with overgrown plants, unwanted weeds and shrubs that had to be cleared in order to enable the land to produce a good crop. Though it looked like a daunting task, the family never faced a challenge they couldn't overcome. They knew the land would change the course of their lives, once they had put in the work. And they were right.

Once they invested an incredible amount of sweat and hard work, the place was completely transformed. In fact, by the end of the first year they harvested a bumper crop of wheat, vegetables and fruits, and the outcome grew better each year thereafter.

In times of shortage, the farm is the place to be, because city people suffer the lack of food and other basic necessities, especially in times of war and ongoing economic depression. Those in the city, find work to be scarce, and food even scarcer, even for those who have money to buy it.

But if you live on a farm, there's always food available, because you can grow your own vegetables and hunt or fish on your own land. My mother made the best cheese in the whole world and baked her own delicious homemade bread, and of course their chickens always laid eggs. And there was always a store of delicious home-brewed wine.

Coffee was rarely used except to treat headaches, instead of aspirin. Homemade pasta was abundant, along with sauce made from fresh-picked tomatoes, herbal spices and meatballs that made wonderful plates of pasta. Life didn't get any better than that.

When they moved to Tossicia, the family included my father and mother, my dad's mother Elisabetta, (Dad's father Antonio had passed away before the family moved to Montorio) and five children, Elisabetta, Maria, Antonio, Luciano, and Nella. Within a few more years, they added three other children to the family—my sister Ester, myself (Moses) and Samuel.

I immensely enjoyed living and working on the farm, because there were always things to do, especially if you had younger brothers to play with.

The farm's owner, Mr. Gino Montauti, was thrilled with the amazing transformation of the land and the vast amount of crops it produced, as well as my father's impressive reputation in the community. The farm was, by then, a showplace Mr. Montauti could be proud of. To show his gratitude, he gave my father his blessing, as well as the rarely-bestowed responsibility for the running of the farm in any way he wanted. My parents responded with great enthusiasm. Things couldn't have turned out better.

The owner's gratitude inspired him to name them his "Sharecropper family' and offer them the privilege of staying on the farm as long as they wanted.

We stayed on the farm at Tossicia for twenty-six years, from 1934 to 1960 when my father's dream was finally realized, and he moved the whole family to his beloved Canada. In total, they had been in Italy for thirty-eight years. Fourteen family members had already emigrated to Brantford, Ontario, Canada, by the time my parents finally boarded an Air Canada plane in the summer of 1960. After eight hours in the air, they landed at the Pearson International Airport in Toronto, and my father knelt and literally kissed the ground, thanking God that he was finally home.

During our time in Italy, things were pretty good on the farm, because everyone shared in the hard work, including the children and our grandmother.

The neighboring farmers began to recognize that there was something unique and different about the family. As a result of their hard work, the place was now lush and green, flourishing even during a severe drought, when other farms were failing. Our land produced more crops per acre, and of far better quality than those of other farms. Even the livestock was healthy and thriving.

Neighboring farmers couldn't hide their curiosity; they wanted to know what made the Di Sabatino farm so successful, so they began to study and replicate the way the family plowed, seeded and harvested their crops. But even with all that effort, they struggled and failed to match the remarkable results of their most successful neighbors.

In the end, they all ended up questioning my dad about his unprecedented success on the farm. That gave Dad an opening to share the gospel, and testify that they had become servants of the Most High God, and that when they had put their trust in God, He made them successful beyond their wildest dreams, infusing them with strength to work hard, and making the land far more fertile, and producing a crop that was excellent in both quantity and quality. He made it clear that it was God's blessing that made all the difference. As you can well imagine, it was a teachable moment; they wanted to know more about this God, whom the family served with such passion.

At that time, my uncles Nicola and Eugenio and their families, lived only a couple of kilometers from our farm, so our three families got together to hold church services, meeting once or twice a week to worship, study the Bible and sing hymns. My father invited the neighbors to join the family for worship, but few accepted the invitation, even after learning that it was Giuseppe's secret for successful farming. Some even took offense and began to mock the Christians, calling them "the evangelists." The rest of the community was made up entirely of Catholics, who now considered Christian teaching unforgiveable. Giuseppe's family was heartbroken, realizing that they were outright rejecting the gospel of salvation and the access to eternal life and peace in the here and now.

Though the brothers faced ridicule and criticism, they continued to share the love of God and invite their neighbors to get to know the Savior.

Though the economy had improved somewhat, people were still struggling to get by, when rumors of impending war created fear and dread in the community.

As a result of the tension, the government forbade groups from meeting, so that meetings of any kind were suddenly against the law. That edict forced the church to go underground, which meant meetings were held at night after dark. Though they were careful, they were soon discovered holding meetings, and were turned into the authorities, who threatened them with fines and possible jail sentences.

My father explained that they were people of peace, and that their meetings were held only to worship God and were not a threat to the government. Dad invited the police chief, who was known as the Maresciallo, to attend services, to see for himself that they were no threat. The man accepted the invitation, was satisfied by what he saw, and gave my father permission to hold meetings, but told him to be more discreet.

My father thanked him for understanding and invited him to continue to attend services, and in the process the chief of police accepted Jesus as Lord and Savior.

In spite of the local opposition, the Lord was working on the hearts of the people, and under the conviction of the Holy Spirit one gentleman accepted the Lord as his personal Saviour and began to attend the church services, and it wasn't long before his entire family got saved and began to rejoice and praise God, and growing in the Lord.

Soon another family got saved and was added to the church. In spite of the recession, threat of war, and the lack of life's necessities, the church was growing.

The evangelism work spread to villages, both near and far, including Forca Di Valle/ Varano, some 5-6 Km away, and both Chermignano/Troiano and Bisenti, were locate 25-30 Km. away.

As people were saved in these villages, the work became too much for my dad, so he recruited capable leaders chosen from among the newly formed "churches" to take care of the day-to-day needs, as well as to lead prayer meetings and Bible studies, and to train the new converts.

In Chermignano-Troiano-Bisenti he assigned Rocco Massimi as the leader of those groups.
In Forca di Valle-Varano, he assigned Domenico Scaccia.

These men served well for a long time and helped to relieve some of the weight of my dad's responsibilities.

An example of my father's weekly agenda:
Monday evening, Bible study/prayer meeting at our house.

Tuesday: travel to Chermignano/Troiano/Bisenti; he would spend two days there.

Thursday: Forca di Valle/Varano; it took only one day as it was closer to home.

Saturday evening: prayer/Bible study meeting at our house.

Sunday: regular church service, held at our home; it was attended by several people from Forca/Varano group as it was a closer to home.

Once a month the churches would meet at our home on Sunday for worship and fellowship and to share testimonies and take the Lord's Supper.

As you can imagine, it wasn't long before the remaining group outgrew the confines of our small home, so the church formed a committee to search for a larger place. They found a small hall in the center of the village of Tossicia, right next to the Catholic Church; it was large enough to accommodate 100-150 people, though it had to be renovated and cleaned up before it could welcome worshippers.

The renovation was done and finished just in time for the inauguration of the new church.

Our church is in beyond the door marked with the red arrow in the picture above.

At the inaugural service, the church was nearly at capacity. Special speakers were invited for the occasion, such as Gioacchino Toppi, pastor of the church in Rome, Giovanni Ferri, a recently converted Catholic priest, and many others, who all joined in the worshiping and rejoicing, young and old, with full enthusiasm and fervor, taking communion, singing hymns and praising and thanking the Lord for establishing such a wonderful place of worship.

This was a fulfillment of God's call on my father's life as Jesus promise in Matthew 28: 19-20:

[18] *Then Jesus came to them (the disciples) and said, "All authority in heaven and on earth has been given to me.* [19] *Therefore go and make disciples of all nations, baptizing them in the name of the Father and of the Son and of the Holy Spirit,* [20] *and teaching them to obey everything I have commanded you. And surely I am with you always, to the very end of the age."*

The work continued and the Lord added to the church those who were being saved.

Trials, Tribulations, Tests, Victories
AND MIRACLES

During those years, my parents endured great suffering and tested to the max.

In 1937, Italy experienced an epidemic called **diphtheria.*****

Tossicia had an outbreak that hit the neighbouring villages and towns pretty hard; many young people died as the result of this epidemic.

All my brothers and sisters ended up suffering from diphtheria to one extent or another.

*** <u>WHAT IS DIPHTHERIA?</u>

Diphtheria is a serious infection caused by strains of bacteria called Corynebacterium diphtheriae that make toxins (poison). It can lead to difficulty breathing, heart failure, paralysis, and even death.

The most common portals of entry of the diphtheria bacillus are the tonsils, nose, and throat. The bacillus usually remains and propagates in that region, producing a powerful toxin that spreads throughout the body via the bloodstream and lymph vessels and damages the heart and the nervous system.

The toxin kills cells in the mouth, nose and throat. The dead cells quickly build up and form a membrane which can attach to the throat and lead to death by choking and suffocation.

Throughout history, diphtheria has been one of the most feared infectious diseases. Epidemics in the United States and Europe resulted in case fatality rates as high as 40%.

Diphtheria was a major cause of childhood mortality before the availability of the diphtheria vaccine.

During that time, the family doctor made his daily trek to the Di Sabatino home to check on the sick kids, and every morning the prognosis grew worse. My parents were exhausted from caring for their severely ill children.

Finally, my mother "had had enough" and decided to have a talk with the Lord. She got on her knees and the prayer went something like this: "Hey God? You know that I am very tired mother. I did all I could to help prevent this sickness, and now I need to turn this situation and my kids over into your hands. My children belong to you, but give me back those that belong to me. Amen."

The next morning, the children woke one by one, and they were all completely healed with the exception of Elisabetta. When she woke, she said to Mom, "Jesus came to me last night and told me He's going to take me home to be with Him, so you don't need to pray for me anymore. I'm going to see my Jesus whom I love, with all my heart."

How does one deal with such stunning news?

There aren't enough words in the dictionary to explain the anguish in a grieving mother's heart. Only the love of God can give peace that surpasses all understanding to ease that kind of pain.

When the doctor made his next home visit, he saw the children out running around and he cried out in a loud voice, **"For sure God has been here!"** (He wasn't a believer.)

After a short visit with the kids, he declared them healed, and gave them a clean bill of health, with the exception of Elisabetta.

A couple of days later, Jesus came to take Elisabetta home to heaven, just as she had told my mother days earlier. She was fourteen years of age at the time.

This was my parents' second most difficult trial; the first was the natural infant death of their three-month old son, Guido.

There is a quote that says: ***"No parent should have to bury a child."*** My parents buried three precious children.

<u>ESTER,</u> the seventh child born to my parents, was born after Nella and before I was born.

She was a bubbly little girl, who showed remarkable intelligence, and exceptional talent. Even at an early age, she could carry on incredibly intelligent conversations.

Ester was of course, loved and adored by my parents and her siblings, but sister Nella was her dearest and favorite sister; they enjoyed a special bond of love.

At twenty-seven months old, she had a terrifying and terrible farm accident, when she suffered third degree burns to a large part of her body. My parents tried everything they could to alleviate her pain, but there wasn't much they could do. Even while lying on her little bed in great pain, she remained calm, encouraging Mother not to cry, and saying, "Jesus is helping me with the pain."

Unfortunately, emergency medical aid wasn't readily available those days; the closest emergency hospital was some 30-35 KM away, so it was four to five hours before they could arrive.

The local family doctor was also notified; he arrived as soon as he could, and after the examination he told them the bad news. All he could do was give her medication to ease the pain.

In the meantime, she remained in bed for 2 more days, never complaining, but instead sang songs of praise to the Lord.

The family was gathered around her tiny bed, praying and waiting on the Lord for a miracle when she asked Mom and Dad to come closer because her voice was growing increasingly faint. She told them that she'd had a visit from Jesus and He told her He was going to take her home to heaven that very day.

Minutes later she asked if everybody was there; she especially asked for "Nanel" which is the name she called her sister, Nella. Nanel wasn't there, so she asked Mom to call her in, saying, "I want everybody to be here when Jesus comes to take me home."

Soon the room filled with the audible sounds of a celestial choir singing stunningly beautiful songs never before heard. It filled the hearts of those in attendance, with unexplainable love, filled each one with a radiant inner glow, as she told each family member goodbye.

As she was still speaking, her voice, the music, and the singing began to fade away to silence.

Ester had slipped away to eternity in the arms of Jesus and the attending angels.

The family was left in awe at God's greatness in that incredible moment.

That was the third terrible trial—losing another child to death.

It was the ultimate "test of all tests" for my parents. A test is defined as:

"Something hard to bear physically or emotionally."

"A state of pain or anguish that tests one's resiliency and character."

"A test of faith, patience, or stamina through subjection to suffering or temptation."

James 1:12 says "Blessed is the man/woman who perseveres under trial, because, when he has stood the test, he will receive the crown of life that the Lord has promised to those who love him."

After Elisabetta's death, there were only four remaining Di Sabatino children: Maria, Antonio, Luciano and Nella. Then on January 2, 1940, three years after Ester's death my mother gave birth to me, a "beautiful baby boy", whom my father named Moses after the great, godly leader of the Jews. Two years later, my brother Samuele was born and was named after a judge, prophet and anointer of kings in Scripture.

The following are details of the life of my parents from the year 1940, the year I was born, as recounted by my parents and siblings.

I was born January 02, 1940 shortly after the start of World War 2. (The war broke out on September 1, 1939.)

During and after the war years, even amid the visible damage sustained in battle, the church grew by leaps and bounds, with many people being saved and added to the church who were looking for comfort and encouragement in spite of the chaos going on around them.

Roundup

A word about the atrocities committed around the end of the war during the so-called ***ROUNDUP.***

*"A **ROUNDUP** was a widespread Nazi World War II security and economic exploitation tactic used in occupied countries, German troops took captive at random thousands of civilians on the streets of subjugated cities. The civilians were captured in groups of unsuspecting passers-by or kidnapped from selected city quarters that had been surrounded in advance by Nazi forces."*

Sant'Anna di Stazzema Massacre

On the morning of August 12, 1944, German troops of the 2nd Battalion of SS Panzergrenadier Regiment 35 of 16th SS Panzergrenadier Division *Reichsführer-SS*, commanded by SS-*Hauptsturmführer* Anton Galler, entered the mountain village of Sant'Anna di Stazzema. With them came some fascists of the 36th Brigata Nera *Benito Mussolini* based in Lucca, dressed in German uniforms.[6]

The soldiers immediately proceeded to round up hundreds of villagers and refugees, locking them in several barns and stables, before systematically executing them.

The killings were done by groups of soldiers carrying machine guns or by herding the detainees into basements and other enclosed spaces and tossing in hand grenades. At the 16th-century local church, the priest Fiore Menguzzo (awarded the Medal for Civil Valor posthumously in 1999[7]) was shot at point-blank range, after which machine guns were then turned on some 100 people gathered there. In all, the victims included at least 107 children (the youngest of whom, Anna Pardini, was only 20 days old[8]), as well as eight pregnant women (one of whom, Evelina Berretti, had her stomach cut with a bayonet and her baby pulled out and killed separately[9]).

After other people were killed throughout the village, their corpses were set on fire (at the church, the soldiers used its pews for a bonfire to dispose of the bodies). The livestock were also exterminated and the whole village was burned down. All this took three hours. The SS men then sat down outside the burning Sant'Anna and ate lunch.

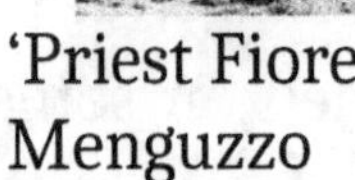

'Priest Fiore
Menguzzo

The reason I bring up the ROUNDUP events is because my father and I were caught up in one of these predicaments.

I was born right after the death of my older sister Ester, which meant that I became kind of a "replacement" for Ester, though my father clearly adored me. In fact, he called me his "precious" and beloved son, and he would take me with him as often as he could, wherever he went. As you can imagine, I followed him with great delight, enjoying every bit of time with him.

One day when I was five years old, my father asked me if I wanted to go with him to the nearby village of Tossicia and I agreed. But as soon as we got to the main road, we saw a massive military truck coming toward us. When it drew near, it came to a sudden stop, and two angry looking German soldiers pulled me and my father into their truck—the biggest truck I'd ever seen up to that point. I was terrified. Of course, at that age everything looked huge and scary.

After driving for a few minutes, we arrived in the town square of Tossicia, where those in charge realized I was of no use to them and let me go, but they continued to hold my father. After a very intense interrogation, where they learned that he could speak English, but was no threat, they released him and let him go. As we later learned, his release was definitely a God thing.

We learned the following morning that the army truck with the 49 remaining men, proceeded to Pescara, a small city situated on a beautiful Adriatic Sea coast, about 30-40KM from Tossicia, where they camped for the night.

The following morning, they rounded up another man to replace my father as the fiftieth man, and right after sunrise they lined them up against a wall and executed them by firing squad in full view of the horrified townspeople.

You may wonder about the significance of the number fifty. For every German soldier found slain, they would round up 50 Italian men at random and execute them by firing squad, (50 to 1). *{You talk about war atrocities...}*

Life After
WORLD WAR 2

Italian industry (in particular iron and steel) was severely damaged **during the war**. Agriculture had also suffered greatly, especially in Central Italy. Major segments of railroads and harbors had been destroyed, and many Italian cities had been bombed and were in ruins. After the war, unemployment rates rose and the value of the "lira", the Italian currency, collapsed.

In a single year, from 1945 to 1946, the cost of goods doubled; the cost of living spiked twenty times higher than it was in 1938. Economic recovery was slow; the transition to "peace-time" industry was painstaking, and there were virtually no commodities to be had. Food rationing engendered a black market for goods and services, and particularly food. Once the Marshall Plan was initiated, American funds were funneled in to help spur the economy in Italy. However, its effects only began to impact the economy in 1953, once Italy had slowly begun to rebuild its economy.

After the **war**, recovery was difficult. **Italy's** towns and businesses had to be completely rebuilt, both physically and socially. But eventually, Italy got back on its feet and became one of the most powerful democracies in the world.

As previously mentioned, the Di Sabatino family wasn't as deeply affected as those in urban areas, because farmers were far more self-sufficient than city-dwellers.

During the recovery years, life seemed to take on a different dimension, when people felt more optimistic about the future. By then, people were ready to move on, leaving the past in the past.

The church community also rallied with new vigor, when several young people between the ages of fourteen and twenty-two, beginning with my brothers and sisters, my cousins, and many others, decided to search the Scriptures and hold weekly prayer meetings to pray for guidance, wisdom and to seek the Lord's will for their lives and the life of the church.

After several weeks of seeking God and praying, the Lord moved in a marvelous way so that they experienced exactly what happened in Joel 2:28-29-32 and Acts 2: 1-4.

"And afterward, I will pour out my Spirit on all people.

Your sons and daughters will prophesy, your old men will dream dreams, your young men will see visions. Even on my servants, both men and women, I will pour out my Spirit in those days. And everyone who calls on the name of the LORD *will be saved. (Joel 2:28-29)*

...they were all together in one place. Suddenly a sound like the blowing of a violent wind came from heaven and filled the whole house where they were sitting.

All of them were filled with the Holy Spirit and began to speak in other tongues as the Spirit enabled them. (Acts 2: 1-4)

In response to their prayers, our young people experienced the Pentecostal** infilling of the Holy Spirit, evidenced by speaking in other languages as the Lord enabled them.

This was the promise Jesus made to the disciples as we find in Acts 1: 4, 5 & 8.

⁴ On one occasion, while he (Jesus after the resurrection) was eating with them, he gave them this command: "Do not leave Jerusalem, but wait for the gift my Father promised, which you have heard me speak about. ⁵ For John baptized with water, but in a few days, you will be **baptized with the Holy Spirit."**

⁸ ... you will **receive power when the Holy Spirit comes on you***; and you will be my witnesses in Jerusalem, and in all Judea and Samaria, [in Tossicia (my version)] and to the ends of the earth."*

** A word about the Pentecostal movement. In 1906, a man by the name of Giacomo Lombardi had a Pentecostal experience when the Azusa Street revival came to Chicago. In 1908 he returned to Italy with the message of Pentecost. As he preached, churches were formed in Calabria, in Abruzzi, (Tossicia is in the province of Abruzzi) and in Rome. Those messages then spread throughout the land, but especially in the South.

**Pentecostalism is unlike any other religious denomination—because it's a mighty move controlled by the Holy Spirit alone, once He's allowed the freedom to move.**

It is the freedom that brings it to life, once a believer asks the Holy Spirit into his life, so that He can operate through a willing servant. Life begets life. Transformed people share their faith, and when others see the power and love of a real true and living God, they too want to be part of that move.

Lombardi did not accomplish all this by himself. In his ministry he was joined by numerous others (returning Italian emigrants) who shared the same experience. The work thrived until 1934 when Fascist persecution began (Winehouse 1-1959:112).

Even during its early years of fantastic growth, Pentecostalism in Italy was not without opposition. The spread was so rapid as to alarm one particular pope, who apparently overstated the case in speaking of Pentecostals as "that movement (which) has invaded every parish of our blessed country" (Evens 1963:280). Protestantism certainly wouldn't have provoked such a reaction, for they were neither as numerous nor as assertive as Pentecostals.

Mussolini's arrival created great difficulties for the Pentecostals. With the signing of the Lateran Pacts, the Vatican was able to appeal to the State to take measures against Protestants. The regime was severe in its dealings with Pentecostals, who were prohibited from meeting. It was against the law to hold services, and offending pastors were sent to prisons or even concentration camps. Pentecostal believers resorted to secret meetings held "in caves, cellars, or in private homes behind barred doors" (Winehouse 1959: I 12). Those difficult days were described to me by some who met in open fields where the grain was high enough to hide behind, and some met in other unusual places. A missionary shared the remarkable story of a "Pentecostal" dog that stood guard while believers met secretly for worship. Only persons who knew the password could get past the dog, and since the Pentecostal greeting "Pace" (peace), which was the password, was not generally known to the police, the system worked well for some time (Hedlund 1970:157).

Mussolini's reign of terror ended in 1944. Under the Allied occupation Pentecostals were finally able to worship freely (Winehouse 1959:11?). Then, from 1949 to 1959, came another period of persecution (Consiglio 1967:72). During this time the Assemblies fought for legal recognition. Finally, in 1959, with the intervention of the Federal Council of Churches, the Assemblies of God were granted the required legal status, and the persecution ended.

The Pentecostal denomination is now more than twice the size of all other Protestant denominations combined. This amazing achievement occurred within the short span of only fifty years. Pentecostals have become the bright spot in Italy in terms of evangelism and church growth. Most Pentecostals are affiliated with the Italian Assemblies of God with its headquarters in Rome. This denomination is tied to its sister organization in the United States, but "with the ties of fellowship only" (Winehouse 1959:17). The Italian Assemblies of God is an autonomous denomination in Italy. I would conservatively estimate 120,000 members in their churches, or an average of 166 members per congregation.

The Assemblies of God in Italy still represents the most consistent Pentecostal Evangelical movement, followed by other associated or federated Evangelical Christian Churches of Pentecostal faith (such as "FCP" and "ACCEI") and many other independent churches. The ADI are made up of 1151 churches, groups and evangelization stations (373 in the North and 703 in the South), conducted by 522 ministers of worship enrolled in the "General Role of Ministries. The work of evangelization is carried out by individual believers and communities also through television with the *Program Cristiani Oggi,* broadcast by 21 broadcasters (one of them on satellite), by the 38 "Radioevangelo" and by the Internet, throughout the nation. Education and information are carried out through Sunday school and the monthly "Christians Today" and "Pentecostal Awakening" programs.

In 1949, the church of Tossicia, including the affiliate groups my father oversaw,
experienced an unusual revival.**+**

+ *{***"Revival** *is a season of **unusual** divine visitation resulting in deep repentance, supernatural **renewal,** and sweeping reformation in the Church, along with the radical conversion of sinners in the world, often producing moral, social, and even economic change in the local or national communities."}*

During that time a stunning transformation swept through the church: *worship services were more vibrant, with renewed energy and enthusiasm, and young people took on new challenges, such as learning to play musical instruments to be used in worship services. A brand-new hunger was created to read and study the scriptures (the Bible), and to witness to people about their need for a personal Savior.

In the process the church had an unusual divine visitation that resulted in deep repentance, supernatural renewal, and a radical conversion of sinners.

*A usual Christian worship service begins with an opening prayer, followed by hymn singing, some testimonies of miracles and healings and the way the Lord changed their lives, then the preaching /sermon, usually by the pastor, as well as an invitation to accept Christ as personal Savior, and closing with prayer.

Such was the case at the village of Forca Di Valle, when Domenico Scaccia and his wife Serafina Scaccia, came in contact with my father, wanting to know about this *"new religion"* he had heard about.

My father met with them, explained the way of salvation, then both Domenico and Sarafina and their son and daughter accepted the Lord as their personal Savior.

The *good news* spread like a "wild fire" and within a short time many from the village and surrounding area also accepted the Lord, so that the increasing number of converts required a larger venue, so the Scaccia family **offered** their home, and a church was birthed at Forca di Valle.*

Farca DI Valle is a small picturesque village with a population of approximately 200, perched on a very steep slope, and retains notable characteristics of antiquity, flanked by modest houses in local stone, some of which may even date back to the 15th - 16th century .

The ancient town is located at 900 meters above sea level, right at the base of the Grand Sasso mountain.

At one of those services a nine-year-old girl by name Maria Pia, a niece of the Scaccia family, (*14 years later she became my wife*) accepted the Lord as her personal Savior, and when she got home, she told her mother of the decision she had made at the service at her uncle Scaccia's place.

The next service the mother attended the service with her daughter, and she too accepted the Lord.

Maria's father Annunzio was away a lot for work, sometimes for a period of two-three weeks or longer, but when he returned home, he noticed a change in the lives of his wife and daughter, who explained their new relationship with Christ. At the next service, he too accepted Christ and was added to the church.

Now, the Catholic Church, the only other church in the village, took note and became incensed that it was losing so many of its parishioners. As a result, the priest took things into his own hands and concocted a plan to quell the loss of its members.

He rallied the people, especially the village youth, with a plan to fight the *"evangelisti", which is how they referred to the unwelcome newcomers. In fact, he ordered the youth to do what they could to disrupt the services and stop the new move of God.*

The case of the three Reggimenti brothers.

During one church service, three brothers, Paolo, Rogantino and Felice Reggimenti were roaming around the area where the service was held with the intent of disturbing the service in order to fulfill the "mandate of the Catholic priest." At that time my oldest brother Antonio was sitting at the back of the church, beside the exit when he saw the three youths, went outside and asked if he could help. When they didn't respond, he invited them to the service.

However, when they stopped to listen to the preaching, the Holy Spirit spoke directly to their hearts, so that they fell to their knees, confessing their sins, and giving their hearts to the Lord.

Afterward they testified that the priest had masterminded the move to disturb and interrupt the service.

From that very moment, the lives of the three young men were completely transformed from "persecutors of the church to preachers of the gospel."

Moved by the Spirit of God, Paolo moved to a suburb of Rome, became a pastor of a local church, and was known as "the walking Bible," because he had a tremendous gift, the ability to recite incredible numbers of scripture verses from memory. He later served as the General Secretary/Treasurer of the Italian Assemblies of God.

Rogantino also moved to Rome, and became a very active member of his church.

Felice also moved away, relocating to another community in the Pescara area, where he started a new work in his home and later established a church in that area of the country.

At Forca di Valle, the work continued and the Lord added to the church those who were being saved.

The case of Andrea Verzilli.

Andrea Verzilli lived approximately 1-2 Km Southeast of Forca di Valle with his large family on a small "gentleman farm" that produced food enough to keep his family fed.

One day one of his sons accidentally got some quicklime powder in his eyes. Realizing it was an emergency, his father rushed him to the doctor, who gave Andrea the bad news — there was no hope for the sight in that eye.

The doctor did what he could, putting ointment on the affected eye, before covering it with a patch and sending them home.

Early the next morning, Andrea consulted my father, told him of the accident, and asked my father to go with him to pray that God would heal his son's eye.

Andrea was well aware of the exhortation by the apostle James, Jesus' brother, in his letter to the churches in James 5:15: chapter 5 verses 14-16: ***And the prayer offered in faith will make the sick person well;***

Later that morning, my father made his way to the son's home and prayed in the name of Jesus for the eye to be healed. Instantly, the young man's eye was completely healed and his eyesight restored.

The Case
OF GIANNINA DI PIETRO

Giannina was a young girl who lived with her parents. She had recently accepted the Lord as her personal Saviour and began to attend the local church my father had established in the village of Troiano, Bisenti.

She faithfully attended the weekly services where she began reading and studying the scripture and devoting time to prayer; as result she was growing in faith and in the knowledge of God.

At the age of fourteen, Giannina had taken a severe fall down a stairway, which left her with lung damage. Over time she developed asthma and struggled with recurring bouts of pneumonia. The problem was severe enough that her doctor advised to stay out of high humidity and wet weather, because the dampness aggravated her lung problems, and could ultimately cause her death.

Moses, Maria Pia, Giannina and husband

Maria Pia, Giannina and Moses

A word about pneumonia

The effects of **pneumonia** on the lungs involve overproduction of mucus and other fluids that accumulate as the result of inflammation and infection, either bacterial or viral, and cause difficulty breathing. In the long term, pneumonia is associated with permanent lung damage, putting people at risk of respiratory failure because the lungs are no longer able to provide oxygen to vital organs. Untreated, pneumonia can lead to chronic obstructive pulmonary disease and eventually, to death.

One day, as she was studying the scriptures she came across a verse in Mark 16:15-18 that says: Jesus said to the disciples … "Whoever *believes and is baptized will be saved, but whoever does not believe will be condemned*" … *"In my name"*… Jesus continued… *"You, (the disciples") will place your hand on the sick people, and they will get well."*

So she made the decision to follow the Lord's command to be baptised*, and risked exposing her lungs to water, which was against her doctor's order. She also knew that the Lord could heal her of her infirmity, so she decided to be baptized at the next baptismal service.

* <u>A word about water baptism</u>

Water baptism is an act of faith and **obedience** to the **commands of Christ**. In Matthew 28:19-20, we find this statement, which establishes it as a doctrine:

"Therefore, (this is Jesus' command to his disciples) go and make disciples of all nations, <u>baptizing them</u> in the name of the Father and of the Son and of the Holy Spirit, and teaching them to obey

everything I have **commanded you**. *And surely I am with you always, to the very end of the age."*

Baptism is a public declaration that you are a follower of Jesus Christ. It is a public confession of your faith in, and commitment to, Jesus Christ. It follows repentance, the confession of sin, and acceptance of the blood sacrifice Christ made in our place. It is an important foundation for the Christian life. Water baptism is a practical demonstration of a spiritual reality that has already taken place in your life, a symbol to identify with the death, burial, and resurrection of Jesus Christ.

The next baptismal service was scheduled for December 25th on Christmas day.

So, when the day came, there were about 25 people in line to be baptized, most of them youths, including Giannina and many guests from their sister churches, to celebrate the occasion, with prayer and testimonies of healings, singing songs and hymns of praise, expressing gratitude to the Lord for the born again experience.

Finally, toward the end of the service, my father began to baptise, nineteen-year-old Giannina, who already looked pale and sickly, and struggled to breathe, when she was helped into the big tub, specially constructed for the occasion and filled with water.

My father baptised her by totally immersing her in the water, and as soon she was helped out of the water, **the miracle happened**. She started to jump with joy shouting: **"I AM HEALED! I AM HEALED!"** In that moment, her appearance changed instantaneously, so that she no longer looked pale or ill, but regained her natural pink color. She was excited when she testified that she had been chronically ill with a deadly disease, but now she was well, because Jesus healed her.

She went on to say, "I am firmly determined and declare today that, to die or to live I am a follower of Jesus Christ my Savior and my Lord, and today I commit my life to follow HIM the rest of my life." Giannina's healing was confirmed and certified by the family doctor.

This was an incredible testimony of how the Lord not only saves but is also Jehovah Rapha, the Lord who heals. In fact, no one in attendance could deny the evidence of the miracle of the HEALING they saw that day, especially on the day we celebrate the birth of our Savior, the

Lord Jesus Christ

Many people came to accept the Lord as the result of seeing the incredible miracle of a living God.

In the end, the Lord granted Giannina a long life, leaving behind a powerful legacy of her faithful service to the Lord, she could truly identify with the scripture verse of 2 Timothy 4: 7-8:

I have fought the good fight, I have finished the race, I have kept the faith, Now there is in store for me the crown of righteousness, which the Lord, the righteous Judge, will award to me on that day—and not only to me, but also to all who have longed for his appearing."

Giannina passed away at the age of eighty-two.

The Case of Filomena Giancola

Filomena was the wife of Domenico Giancola, who lived with their four children on the outskirts of Tossicia; the family was part of the church and were involved in ministry there. In fact, Domenico would fill the pulpit in my father's absence.

Over a period of time Filomena became ill, but the doctor had no answers, and her health continued to deteriorate. It wasn't long before she was bedridden, and near death.

One Sunday morning she turned blue and could no longer speak, and her worried husband was desperate for answers, so he headed to the church, five minutes away and requested that my dad go and pray for his wife.

Domenico was also well aware of the exhortation in James 5:14-16: that the prayer offered in faith will make the sick person well.

My father told Domenico he would visit their home and pray for his wife, but only after the church service ended.

After the service I accompanied my father, and we were led into a room where Filomena was lying in bed, completely unresponsive.

My father prayed a rather short, simple prayer asking God to heal Filomena in the name of Jesus.

He had scarcely ended his prayer when she actually moved for the first time in several days. In that moment, we also saw color return to her pale face just before she sat up and asked for something to eat.

As a nine-year-old boy, I was eyewitness to her instant healing. I was stunned at the power of God, and my faith grew by leaps and bounds as I witnessed such amazing miracles.

Before leaving for home, we rejoiced and praised God with the family for restoring her to excellent health. In the end, she lived forty more years after her healing.

The Case of Franco.

Franco lived in a small village with his wife and their small family, but work was so scarce that he had to take a job as a **shepherd**, just outside of town.

A shepherd or sheepherder is a person who tends, feeds, or guards herds of sheep owned by a wealthy person or corporation that owns thousands of sheep that are raised for their milk and meat, but especially for their wool.

This type of work often required the shepherd to be away from his family, sometimes for a period of two to three weeks, and sometimes even longer, putting a strain on family life.

Franco's family were religious people of Roman Catholic faith, but in reality, that had no impact on their everyday lives. In fact, there was no room for

God, which left them feeling empty, restless and dissatisfied. Franco himself was possessed by a spirit of torment that was actually driving him mad. He had come to the end of his road.

One day when he had time off from work, his friend Domenico invited him to a prayer meeting that was held at Pastor Di Sabatino's home. Desperate for answers, he accepted the man's invitation. That evening the Lord Jesus revealed Himself to Franco in such marvelous way, that he was delivered from the spirit of torment that had continually caused physical pain and mental anguish.

That night he was filled with the kind of love and joy that only God can give. Those in attendance testified that he couldn't stop jumping for joy and praising God for the deliverance, shouting "I am free! I am free!"

That evening, his life was changed forever. When his wife saw the radical change in his life, she too accepted Christ and it wasn't long before even his sons got saved.

*That was one more confirmation that my father was living out God's call on his life. As written in Mark 16:15-18: He said to them (the disciples): "Go into all the world and (**preach**) the gospel to all creation. Whoever believes and is baptized will (**be saved**), but whoever does not believe will be condemned. And these signs will accompany those who believe in my name they will (**drive out demons**) they will speak in new tongues...they will place their hands on sick people, and (**they will get well.**)*

Here we find four distinctive ministries:
1. Go and preach the ***good news: Jesus saves***,
2. Whoever believes and is baptised, will ***be saved***,
3. In Jesus name, drive ***out demons***,
4. When you pray for the sick, they will ***get well.***

Here we see evidence of how the Lord responds to the prayer of faith, through the work of the Holy Spirit:

1. The Reggimenti Brothers were **_saved_** and called into ministry.
2. Andrea Verzilli's son was **_healed_** and his eyesight was restored.
3. Filomena Giancola, received instantaneous **_healing_**; she went from near-death to living a long productive life.
4. Franco was **_delivered_** from a spirit of torment and oppression.

The churches of "Tossicia" were going through a season of revival; people were being saved, healed from their infirmities, delivered of demonic spirits; and the Lord was adding to the church those who were being saved.

As I mentioned in a previous chapter, though God was moving mightily, my parents were going through trials and tribulations, being tested to the max.

To summarise just few of the trials and tests and tragedies:

1. Trying to survive poverty, a family of eight adults, three young married couples and their children as well as two grandparents, lived in an incredibly small house. At one point there were twenty people living there together.
2. Living through the lean years during WW1 and WW2.
3. Living through the Great Depression where scarcity was the rule.
4. Family tragedies, including the death of three children, ages fourteen, three months, and twenty-seven months old.
5. All their children were affected by the diphtheria pandemic, but God stepped in and miraculously healed all but one of them, whom He took home to heaven.

Even when I try, I can't imagine the heartache they faced over the years, yet God was there to comfort, encourage and use them in His grand design plan.

At this point, I want to quote the lyrics of a song by Andrae Crouch, that puts everything in perspective:

<u>Through It All</u>

I've had many tears and sorrows
I've had questions for tomorrow
But in every situation
God gave me blessed consolation.
And I thank him for the storms he brought me through
That my trials come to only make me strong.
Through it all, through it all
I learned to trust in Jesus
I've learned to trust in God
I've learned to depend upon his word
Let me tell you that through it all
I've learned to depend upon his word.

In James 1:12 we read "Blessed is the man/woman who perseveres under trial, because, when he has stood the test, he will receive the crown of life that the Lord has promised to those who love him.

God must have been pleased with my parents for the way they persevered, because they stayed the course. Along the way, they learned that *trials only came to make* them *strong. And as they took Him at His Word, He rewarded them with many victories and miracles.*

Miracles
AND VICTORIES

No doubt you've heard the phrase: **"There is calm after the storm."**_In this instance the storm is defined as:

The period during which things improve after a difficult, chaotic, or stressful time.

"The thing about the storms is that there's always a sense of peace once the storm is over."

That phrase truly describes the time after the trials passed in my parents' lives.

I would need to write another entire book to share all the miracles and God's timely interventions as well as personal and spiritual victories, but I will detail only a few events that took place during and after the church's revival.

Definition of a miracle.

An extraordinary event *manifesting* divine intervention in human affairs.

A divinely natural phenomenon that humans experience as the fulfillment of a spiritual law.

An unusual or wonderful event that is believed to be caused by the power of God.

Miracles on the farm:

I was around the age of ten when I personally witnessed an incredible miracles in a single day.

One day a catastrophic wind storm with loud thunder and torrential rain devastated most of that year's wheat crop in the area, and on our farm.

At the approach of harvest time, it was clearly evident that there was no grain on the stocks, but in faith, my father held out hope for a great harvest in spite of what he saw with his eyes. So, he hired the threshing machines as he had always done.

As you can imagine, those who were watching criticized him for what they believed was a foolish decision.

New grain stocks

Ripen wheat stocks

Check for quality/quantit y

A normal wheat harvest:
Wheat harvesting was always a time of rejoicing, when farmers would exchange manpower, helping each other harvest their crops. It would usually take a crew of ten to fifteen men four to six hours depending on the size of the crop.

After the work was finished, a short celebration would take place with food and drinks, provided by the host farmer.

Pic 1. Wheat neatly in to a pile

Pic 2. Men threshing the wheat

Pic 3. Sacks of grain lined up.

These pictures show the old threashing machinery used in the grain threshing operation.

As a rule, wheat is gathered and made in to a big pile (pic 1) the threshing machine is parked next to the wheat pile, then the wheat is fed into the thresher as seen in the second photo. The thresher would then separate the straw and husk, which was thrown out the front, while the grain would be ejected from the back, and poured into bags that would be weighed and recorded by two individuals. Then the bags would be lined up for further inspections.

You may recall that we didn't own the farm; rather we were sharcroppers where a land owner allows the sharecropper to farm the land in return for a share of the crops produced by the land.

Our landowner, Gino Montauti had learned to trust my father and leave all authority in his hands, which meant that he rarely showed up to check on the process, but he loved to come for grain harvest, so he stopped by and witnessed the incredible miracle of the grain harvest.

That day the grain poured out the back of the threshing machine, filling bag after bag, from a crop that looked like it would produce nothing. Dad's critics watched wide-eyed realizing it had to be God, to produce such an incredible outcome. What a wonderful testimony to God's faithfulness.

Everyone present could see that miracle happening before their very eyes, and no one could doubt that it was a miracle from God. This gave Dad another opportunity to witness about the love and provision of our wonderful Lord. As a result, even more people were saved and added to the growing church. The truth is that nothing encourages the body of Christ like the miracles they see with their own eyes!

Time Out
WITH MY MOTHER, SOFIA

For the last several years of my mother's life, I visited her at least every Tuesday evening,, when we had our usual "date." By that time, she was over eighty and struggling to read, due to failing eyesight, so I would sit and read God's Word to her, and she would pray for me and my family. During those visits she would often share the many ways God had always been there, meeting the needs of our family. And she would never fail to testify that she yearned to love and serve Him to the end.

As part of her testimony, she often made this statement: *"The Lord has been faithful to this day, and the future is in His hands. My hope is in the Lord, He has promised me ETERNAL LIFE, and one day I will be reunited with my Elisabetta, with Guido and with Ester, my children that preceded me to heaven."*

To those of us who know and love Him, we will eventually hear the following glorious words: 'Well *done,* good and faithful servant; you were faithful through your trials and tribulations and family tragedies ... Enter into the joy of your Lord.'

In spite of the hardships, we often ended up singing this song:

What a day that will be, When my Jesus I shall see, And I look upon His face,
The One who saved me by His grace; When He takes me by the hand, And leads me through the Promised Land, What a day, glorious day that will be.
There'll be no sorrow there, No more burdens to bear, No more sickness, no more pain, No more parting over there; But forever I will be,

With the One who died for me, What a day, glorious day that will be.

As we reminisced, even In her late years of her life, (she died at age nighty-one) and she would share how the Lord took Guido, Elisabetta, and Ester, we would often break in to soft weeping at the memories.

Even now I get teary eyed when I think of the day when I meet my Jesus, who will introduce me to my three unknown siblings: Guido, Elisabeth and Ester for the first time.

And once again I will be able to sit down with my mother and the rest of my family to enjoy the beauty of heaven. I can only shout a big THANK YOU, JESUS! for saving my soul and for eternal life.

Other miracles.

Multiplication of bread.

After the end of World War 2, it took time for the country to get back on its feet. Those who lived in large cities suffered more than those in the rural/

farming communities; even if you had the money to buy it, food was very scarce, so that people tended to go to farmers to get produce or whatever they could find, just to survive.

My father had cultivated a friendship with Mr. G.ippoT. (*Not his real name to conceal his identity*) that became his mentor in the way of the Lord; Mr. ippoT was the pastor of the church in Rome at that time. He and his family lived in the city of Rome, the largest city in Italy. In 1950 it boasted a population of approximately 2 million. By 2021 its population had grown to 4.5 million.

Mr. ippoT would make frequent and extended visits to the Tossicia church, (Rome is 150 km. from Tossicia) where he usually stayed for a couple of weeks to preach and lead Bible studies.

At times he brought his wife, and since they stayed at our house, they became part of our extended family.

Whenever they left to go home, my mother would prepare a package of necessities, including food such as homemade bread, cold cuts etc. to take with them, which would help immensely, as food was very scarce in the big city.

At our farm we had our own heart oven that allowed us to make 15-20 large loaves of bread, which would be enough to last two to three weeks at a time; the bread was kept in a container (a large bread box) especially made to keep the bread fresh.

As my mother was preparing the "bundle" for the ippoTs, she asked me to get 2-3 loaves of bread to add to the package, so I went to get the bread from the container, and to my surprise there was only one loaf left, so I took it to Mom, and she asked, *"Why did you get me just one loaf when I asked for 2 or three loaves?"*

My simple answer was *"That's all there is. That was the only loaf left. The bread box is **empty**."*

She asked me to check again, and when I did, I returned with the same answer.

So, she made the trip to the box and as she lifted the lid, she was surprised and pleased to see that the container was **full to the brim**. She started to praise the Lord in Italian and in another language I could not understand, with both arms lifted toward the ceiling, all I could hear was *"Thank you Lord, thank you Lord, you did it again!"*

The ippoTs took home more than three loaves that day. In the end, God provided so much bread that we didn't have to bake for the next three weeks.

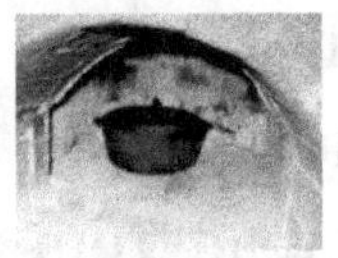

Heart oven

Multiplication of Spaghetti dinner.

From time to time the church at Tossicia would hold a special service inviting believers from other churches to join in celebrating God's goodness, sharing thanksgiving and testimonies of what the Lord had been doing in their lives by singing and praising with special music, and ended with the baptism of new believers and celebrating the Lord's Supper.

On one of these events, we were expecting the special speaker, a group of fifteen young people and their chaperones from the Church of Rome, who finally arrived after nearly seven hours on the road, terribly tired and hungry. They just wanted to eat!

My mother made a quick search of the food supply and found only a single 1 lb. package of spaghetti, which would have been enough for four to five people. So how could she feed such a large group?

However mother didn't panic, she quickly asked my two sisters to find the biggest pot, fill it with water and put it on the fire to boil, and to also find the biggest platter to serve the spaghetti. With the package of spaghetti in her hands, she looked toward heaven and prayed, ***"Hey God? You know the situation here; you know I only have this small package of spaghetti, you see? These people are hungry; You need to feed them, okay God? Amen."***

She put the spaghetti in the pot of boiling water and waited while it cooked.

The air was filled with the aroma of homemade tomato sauce made with fresh-picked tomatoes and olive oil as well *as* parsley, basil, and oregano, which only added to the hungry group's anticipation.

In the meantime, my two older brothers quickly prepared an antipasto with freshly baked bread, sliced prosciutto, some pecorino cheese, and some other cold cuts, which they ate while waiting for the spaghetti.

When the large pot of spaghetti came off the fire, ready to be scooped onto the large platter, (remember, there was only 1 lb. of spaghetti that went in to that large pot) they scooped and scooped the spaghetti, filling the platter to the brim, they had to smile with gratitude when they saw that there still was more spaghetti left in the pot.

All were served a full plate of delicious pasta, and even went back for more, until they were full, with more spaghetti left for another meal.

In the end, God had come through with another miracle, that of the ***multiplication of spaghetti***.

An antic
water boiling
pot

My aunt
dishing up
spaghetti

My wife
serving
spaghetti
dinner.

IDA CINA,
THE CHISTIAN LADY FROM THE USA

As I mentioned in a previous chapter, the work of the Lord spread to other villages, like Forca Di Valle/ Varano, some 5-6 km. away; Bisenti, and Chermignano/Troiano, both 25-30 km. away. My father conducted the services in these places on a weekly basis.

One time, while visiting the group in Bisenti, my father walked to the bus station to take the bus home, only to learn that the bus had just left and there were no other buses for the rest of the day. Why? Because he had no wristwatch, and arrived at the bus station too late.

Pictures of some busses circa 1945/1950

After the end of WW2, transportation was very spotty and unreliable. The main transportation was by bus and that was expensive, however, Dad managed to save enough money to purchase the required ticket in order to visit churches far from home.

At times he'd go to the bus station with no money in his pocket and unexpectedly some total stranger would approach my father, handing him an envelope and suddenly disappearing.

In the envelope he would find the exact amount he needed to purchase the ticket to his destination, realizing that God had sent an angel to provide the money for the ticket.

At the bus station after he missed the bus, he had to decide whether to stay overnight and go home the next morning or take a chance and walk home. He decided to walk home as he had an important meeting the next day.

The distance from the village of Bisenti to our home would require a four to five hour walk if all went well. Since he was familiar with the area, he decided to take "short cuts" through farm country.

After he had walked for an hour or so, the weather changed and it began to drizzle and then storm hard accompanied by fierce thunder and lightning, that soon turned the roads into a morass of mud as the sun set. In the end, the walk that should have taken five hours, took seven hours, because of the terrible storm, but God motivated him to keep walking until he finally made it home.

By the time he had finally arrived, mother and the rest of the family were sleeping, but Leo the Faithful guard dog, was the first to greet Dad, and he grew so excited that he went into a frenzy and managed to wake the whole family.

Everyone was thrilled and relieved that Dad had made it safely home, but concerned because, no sooner was Dad inside the house he collapsed on the floor, overcome by exhaustion.

After a short rest he regained some strength and with Mother's help he cleaned up, changed in to dry clothes then recounted his ordeal while eating a much-needed meal. We listened to the story with such intensity that we actually felt the pain he endured, so deeply that we got on our knees and cried out to God, thanking Him for the incredible way He protected him.

It all happened because he missed the bus, so at the end of his story, my father lamented, "Oh, if I only had a watch!"

(In those days only few people had watches, because they were very costly.)

No long afterward, Dad was notified that there was mail for the Di Sabatinos, at the post office. There he found a substantial number of parcels sent from various churches from the USA addressed to "Giuseppe Di Sabatino, pastor of the Christian Church of Tossicia."

These parcels were sent to churches all over Europe, as the result of the Marshal Plan.

The Marshall Plan was a U.S.-sponsored program that was implemented following the end of World War II. It was intended to aid European countries that had been destroyed as a result of the war.

Inside of one of these parcels there was a little gift box neatly wrapped, and inside was a beautiful silver lady's watch with a letter that read as follows:

"Dear Brother Di Sabatino, while I was in prayer, the Lord spoke to me telling me that in Tossicia Italy was a pastor by name Giuseppe Di Sabatino who was in need of a watch. I was so touched by the voice of God that I had to respond to the need.

"Brother Di Sabatino, I am sending my own watch, this the best I can do for now. I hope this will help you."

Sincerely,
Ida Cina.

 As you can imagine, we were all in tears when we saw the watch.

After reading the letter, we couldn't help but realize how the Lord orchestrated this miracle months earlier by speaking to Ida Cina, a lady from a distant continent of America, a complete stranger.

We stopped to pray and thank Jehovah Jireh—the Lord is our Provider, for answering my dad's prayer even before he prayed. Over time we made several attempts to find this precious faithful lady in order to thank her for the wonderful gift.

My father wore that lady's watch with pride wherever he went, RECOGNIZING THE GIFT GOD provided for him in answer to a prayer of faith in his time of need.

The watch never broke down and served my dad for many long years.

Angel
VISITATION

<u>*Angels! Who are THEY?*</u>

"Angels are <u>***messengers, ministering spirits***</u> sent to serve those who will inherit salvation.
   Hebrews 1:14

Do not forget to show hospitality to strangers, for by so **doing** some people have **shown hospitality** to angels without knowing it.
Hebrews 13: 2

<u>*Abraham entertained angels*</u>

The account is found in Genesis 18:1-8

ANGEL VISITATION

Abraham saw "three men" standing nearby, he offered them some water to wash up... he said to them "Let me get you something to eat so you can be refreshed and then go on your way."

"Very well," they answered, "do as you say."

...Abraham then brought some curds and milk and the calf that had been prepared, and set these before them. **_"While they ate,_** he stood near them under a tree."

Angels ".... **_ate_** at Lot's house".
Genesis 19:3

The angel of the LORD encamps around those who fear him, and he **_delivers_** them.
Psalm 34:7

...He will command His angels concerning you to **_guard_** you in all your ways. For he will order his angels to **_protect_** you wherever you go.
Psalm 91:11, 14

<u>Why?</u> ***<u>"Because he loves you,"</u>*** says the LORD.

My parents were going through a time of turmoil; the farming required more work as we worked to increase the crop production to fulfil the family's needs; the kids were busy with the work on the farm, and also with school work. And because of Dad's increased work load with the churches, he was away for longer periods, leaving Mom and my older brothers to manage the farm. As you can imagine, my mother missed her husband dearly.

So, this created tension between my mom and dad and the family, so my mother took all her burdens, to the Lord in prayer.

This brings to memory a song by **<u>Joseph M. Scriven</u>**

"What a Friend We Have in Jesus"

I'll quote some of the lyrics here:

What a friend we have in Jesus, All our sins and griefs to bear! What a privilege to carry *Everything to God in...*

Have we trials and temptations? Is there trouble anywhere? We should never be discouraged— Take it to the Lord in prayer. Are we weak and heavy-laden, Cumbered with a load of care? Precious Savior, still our refuge— Take it to the Lord in prayer... Blessed Savior, Thou hast promised Thou wilt all our burdens bear; May we ever, Lord, be bringing All to Thee in earnest prayer...

The Lord heard her prayer and soon sent an ANGEL to comfort, encourage, and to pronounce a BLESSING for the family just before he went away.

That day began as usual, the breakfast table was set and ready, the kids rounded up and seated around the breakfast table ready to eat before the day's work began.

As was the custom of that day, the front door of the house was wide open; it was only closed at night, and Leo, our guard dog, was at his post, beside the door, always alert to strangers.

Suddenly a "MAN" walked in the house, totally unnoticed by the dog. My mother greeted him and asked him to stay for breakfast. He accepted and sat between my youngest sister Nella and my mother.

Mother as usual offered a prayer of blessing for the food and protection for the day and also prayed for her husband that the Lord would give him journey mercies and a profitable time with the churches.

We began to eat, this "MAN" **ate** along with us. Soon my mother began to tell him of the frustration she was experiencing with her "pastor husband," "my father", and how his work as a pastor required him to be away from the family more than she preferred, because his fatherly presence and leadership was greatly missed by the family. Over the meal she shared it all.

At that the "MAN" replied, saying, "I KNOW, I KNOW" "I KNOW THAT", "HE IS DOING GOOD WORK" and "HAVE PATIENCE."

Once breakfast ended, the man got up from his seat, asked if all of the family were present, then he raised his hand toward heaven and simply said, (*he spoke Italian*) "MAY the blessing of the Lord be upon YOU (plural) and give you all GOOD HEALTH and God's prosperity *TO YOU AND THE REST OF YOUR FAMILY*, young and old."

Then he walked out the door and instantly disappeared.

We were completely astounded when we realized we'd had a visitation from an angel of the Lord. We could only stand there staring at each other in amazement, realizing that he wasn't a mere man but an Angel sent by God to minister comfort, and to encourage my mother to carry on the work as a Pastor's wife, and the farm management and the growing family and best of all to bless the family not only "the present generation but also the next generation and even the children yet to be born so they would put their trust in God, and not forget his deeds but would keep his commands."

Reflection

I am the second generation, the 8th child of nine born to Giuseppe and Sofia Di Sabatino family;

I can say with confidence that God has kept HIS WORD, in regard to "the blessing the angel of the Lord prayed over our family."

My wife and I were blessed with two wonderful boys Daniel and Sandro.

They are the (third generation), and were both dedicated to the Lord at a very young age. In due time both married wonderful Christian wives, each blessed with children and later were both called into pastoral ministry.

Daniel had been a head pastor to two churches before he was asked to serve as Secretary/Treasurer of the Wester Ontario District of the Pentecostal Assemblies of Canada, a very large district overseeing over 300 churches.

Sandro, after serving as head pastor of relatively large church in Vancouver BC, presently is serving as the head pastor of St. Andrew's International Church in Athens, Greece.

Daniel and wife Kelly were blessed with three boys, Nicholas, Alexander and Zachary (fourth generation) and three grandchildren, (fifth generation).

Sandro and his wife Rebecca were blessed with two boys, Soren and Simeon, and a daughter, Shaiana, (fourth generation).

From left to right:

Nick; Alexander; Kelly, Daniel's wife; Daniel. Me (Moses)

Sandro; Rebecca, Sandro's wife; Soren; Simeon, Shaiana;

Missing in the picture is Daniel's first born Zachary as he and his wife were away at the time this picture was taken.

Also missing in the picture is my wife Maria Pia as she had just passed away a year before this picture was taken.

This is Zachary's family: Zac with Connor, Gloria with Brody and Kristina.

I can truly say the Lord has been faithful and truly blessed the Di Sabatino household.

In the words of Joshua, Moses's aid, the leader and military commander of Israel, as he gives the State Of Government address, he concludes with these words as we find in Joshua 24:15 ..."*Choose for yourselves this day whom you will service,... But as for me and my household, we will serve the Lord*" this verse reverberates throughout the generations of the Di Sabatino clan, and I renew my commitment and declare: **_As for me and my household, we will serve the Lord._**

life after
RETURN TO CANADA

The time had finally arrived for Dad to return to Canada. Thirty eight years had passed since he first had returned to Italy, where he stayed from 1922 to 1960.

By then the entire family had already immigrated to Canada; my parents were the last to arrive to Brantford, Ontario, Canada, my father's beloved city.

We were all anxiously waiting for this day as we knew how deeply my dad longed to reunite with the entire family in CANADA. By that time we were fairly well established in the community, so Mom and Dad moved in with my brother Luciano who was still single. They would be an asset to my brother in helping with household chores, cooking, house cleaning, etc.

It didn't take long for Dad to reconnect with some old friends he had left when he returned to Italy, and of course, they would often sit around a table sipping coffee or a cold pop or a bottle of Brio (the "Italian Coke") and reminisce about "the good old days." Some of their stories were funny, others were serious, and others... well, all the sudden they would just break laughing over something that only they understood; they were really enjoying their time together, now that my dad had come home.

Dad and Uncle Eugenio

Typical Sunday dinner

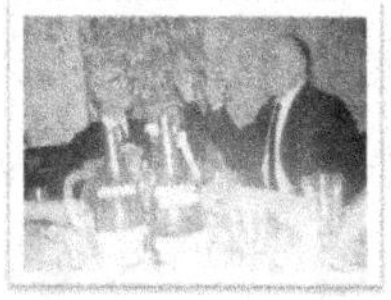

Dad and Uncle Eugenio living it up

One of the things my parents enjoyed most was attending weddings, especially mine.

Moses and Maria Pia   Mom and Dad

It was September 28, 1963, when I married the "most beautiful young lady in the whole wide world" *[of course this is strictly my own opinion].* Maria Pia Verzilli, was originally from Forca di Valle; Maria Pia was the nine-year old girl who accepted the Lord as her personal Savior, after hearing my father preach the message of salvation. And not only did she get saved, but she was also instrumental in witnessing to her parents. (Read her story here below).

"....At one of those services (church service) a nine-year-old girl by name Maria Pia, a niece of the Scaccia family, (14 years later she became my wife) accepted the Lord as her personal Savior, and when she got home, she told her mother of the decision she had made at the service at her uncle Scaccia's place.

The next service the mother attended the service with her daughter, and she too accepted the Lord.

Maria's father Annunzio was away a lot for work, sometimes for a period of two-three weeks or longer, but when he returned home, he noticed a change in the lives of his wife and daughter, who explained their new relationship with Christ. At the next service, he too accepted Christ and was added to the church."

We were honored to have my parents at our wedding, especially when my father prayed for us and spoke a blessing over our lives, then encouraged us to continue to serve the Lord with all our hearts.

My younger brother Samuel married next, to a wonderful girl by the name of Bessie La Mantia. My parents were glad to see another of their sons married.

Samuel and Bessie were honored to have both her parents and mine at their wedding.

The newlywed couple moved to Toronto and took up residence there.

The next wedding was that of my brother Luciano who married Pina Ciardulli. My father had a big part in the ceremony. In fact, he had the honor of walking Pina to the altar. Pina's father had passed away a couple of years earlier, and she had no family nearby, which is why she asked my father to walk her down the aisle. He was, of course, thrilled to participate.

As for the family's life, we had lots family reunions and family picnics. We celebrated as often as we could, just enjoying the company of our parents, who were happiest when they could gather the whole family together to celebrate. Sometime I brought my accordion, someone else brought a guitar, and often we would break out in songs and of course eat lots of ITALIAN food, just having a great time together, thankful the whole family was serving the Lord.

The Italian
PENTECOSTAL CHURCH IN BRANTFORD

The Italian Pentecostal Church in Brantford was started sometime in the early 1950s by the Di Sabatino and the Giancola families along with other immigrants that lived in Brantford prior of the 1950s. As a result of the great influx of the immigrants "between 1950 to 1960" the church was established and quickly grew in members.

The second Wold War left Italy devastated, however by the year 1946/1950 the economy had improved a whole lot but some were still suffering from the effects of the war, so people of all ages emigrated to other countries looking for better life, and Canada became a prime destination.

Between the early 1950s and the mid-1960s, approximately 20,000 to 30,000 Italians emigrated to Canada each year, many of the men taking jobs in the construction industry. Pier 21 in Halifax, Nova Scotia was an influential port of Italian immigration between 1928 until it closed in 1971. A total of 471,940 individuals had come to Canada from Italy, making them the third largest ethnic group to emigrate to Canada during that time period. In the late 1960s, the Italian economy experienced a period of growth and recovery, removing one of the primary incentives for emigration. The importance of Italian Canadians cannot be overstated in the growth of the modern economy. In 2010, the Government of Ontario proclaimed the month of June as Italian Heritage Month, and in 2017, the Canadian Government also declared the month of June as Italian Heritage Month across Canada.

Over the years the church has developed a very well-established identity serving people of many different ethnicities; as they grew the congregations have become increasingly diverse and "less Italian" with each new generation.

The church today operates under the name of New City Church and is part of the Canadian Assemblies of God, one of three Canadian branches of the Assemblies of God, with a common desire to serve and share their passion for God with others.

So, Mom and Dad joined the Italian Pentecostal Church where the rest of the family not only were already members but also the co-founders.

Rosa and Ercole

My cousin Ercole Di Sabatino was the Pastor. *(Ercole was my Uncle Nicola's oldest son).*

Unfortunately, Pastor Ercole Di Sabatino was diagnosed with cancer and passed away at the age of thirty-eight, leaving his wife and three young children as well as a church with no pastor.

The congregation asked my father to be the interim pastor till they found a full-time pastor, which he gladly accepted.

After a diligent search for a full-time pastor, Pastor Rinaldo and wife Leah Remoli, well known to the congregation, were invited to serve as the head pastor of the church, and they gladly assumed the duties of full time pastor.

At last, my parents were able to finally begin a well-deserved retirement, giving them more time to enjoy the grandchildren and spend more time with family and friends.

My father could easily identify with the Apostle Paul when he the Apostle Paul addressed his final instructions "to his true son in the faith, Timothy." With his personal witness and instructions Paul was able to say:

"For I am already being poured out like a drink offering, and the time for my departure is near. I have fought the good fight, I have finished the race, I have kept the faith, Now there is in store for me the crown of righteousness, which the

Lord, the righteous Judge, will award to me on that day—and not only to me, but also to all who have longed for his appearing."
(2 timothy 4:6-8"

My parents lived with my brother Luciano's family until they passed away.

My Father passed away May 30, 1982 at the age of 86.

My Mother passed away January 4, 1993 at age 91.

As I am writing these last lines of my parent's life story, I couldn't help but break into tears of joy singing the hymn below penned by Johnson Oatman: **"When I've gone the last mile of the way,"** it's so applicable to my parents' lives.

> If I walk in the pathway of duty,
> If I work till the close of the day,
> I shall see the great King in His beauty,
> When I've gone the last mile of the way.
> *Refrain:*
> When I've gone the last mile of the way,
> *I will rest at the close of the day;*

<u>And I know there are joys that await me,</u>
When I've gone the last mile of the way.
<u>If for Christ I proclaim the glad story,</u>
If I seek for His sheep gone astray,
I am sure He will show me His glory,
When I've gone the last mile of the way.
Here the dearest of ties we must sever,
<u>Tears of sorrow are seen every day;</u>
<u>But no sickness, no sighing forever,</u>
When I've gone the last mile of the way.
<u>And if here I have earnestly striven,</u>
<u>And have tried all His will to obey,</u>
<u>'Twill enhance all the rapture of heaven,</u>
When I've gone the last mile of the way.

At this point, I can only thank God for my wonderful heritage of faith, and give praise to God who works so miraculously, not only to provide for the needs of His people, but to those watching, who need to see the love of God demonstrated in real time, and to receive the great salvation He offers. Amen and amen!

Dear Reader,

If your life was touched while reading *THE DI SABATINO LIFE STORY*, please let us know!
We would love to celebrate with you!

mdisabatino@outlook.com

In His Presence,
Moses DI SABATINO

www.ingramcontent.com/pod-product-compliance
Lightning Source LLC
Chambersburg PA
CBHW071953150726
47999CB00001B/424